MW00935169

For my Mother who always encouraged me to go on around the corner in life.

# My Gratitude

**Kindred Heart Writers**: Johnnie Alexander, Karen Evans, Laura Groves, Jean Wise. My on-line Writers' group for many years who continue to uplift me in every way.

**Lakeside Bible Study Group**: Carolyn Baker, Glenda Berry, Jane Blair, Joan Brown, Mary Jo Fiser, Connie Houston*, Roseanne Moss*, Patty McHenry, Page Patrick, Mary Catherine St.John, Miriam St.John, Linda Schneider, and Sharon Wacaser. I am convinced their prayers brought this book to the finish.

*Lunch friends, Manuscript Readers and heavy on prodding

**Jeremy and Renae Rinkel, my editors**: I am amazed at the talent Jeremy has to edit and design. He and Renae are an amazing team. I am so thankful to have worked with them as peers and as friends.

# Contents

# 1

# Rest for Your Soul

I really didn't want to get up this morning. My body was achy...nothing major. Just "old-age" aches and pains which usually disappear once I am up and moving. But this morning seemed a good morning to turn on my other side, wrap my arms around my pillow, pull the sheet a little closer to my chin and snuggle down for another few minutes. I knew if I did, my walk wouldn't happen. I promised myself I will walk this week, so I made myself get up, get dressed and start down the blacktop toward the highway. I would not describe my steps as lively or my face as joyful, but I am walking.

I plod along my usual route, and as I turn the corner to start the last lap of my journey, there they are in front of me...right in the middle of the road. A doe and her little fawn also taking their morning stroll. Batting their eyes and twitching their white tails, they stand ears-up alert, poised to run at the slightest indication of danger. Obviously not feeling I am too dangerous, the mother and baby wander slowly across the road, turn once to check me out and then bound into the cornfield behind Crestwood School. The sun is shining, the birds are singing and God's creation is all around me. Watching the deer, I stop for a minute, enjoy my surroundings and thank God that I am physically able to walk as a part of His creation.

I continue towards home thankful I trudged the path and turned the corner to experience the sudden beauty of a mother and her child of nature. Again God reminds me in his own way "this is the day that the Lord has made and I will rejoice and be glad in it" (Psalm 118:24).

I wonder if this isn't also true about our daily spiritual walk. Many times I start the day not anxious to do the God "things" I know I should do. Reading my Bible, praying, calling on the sick, sending the cards, and talking to my neighbor about Jesus are not things I want to do. I would much rather pull the sheet of the world around me and go on with my life of pleasure.

And yet, when I take the time and make the effort, I find many lovely surprises waiting for me as I turn the corner. I realize how God's Word speaks to me so personally and the joy I feel when the day is done. Again His Word comes "Ask where the good way is and walk in it and you will find rest for your soul" (Jeremiah 6:16). May you find rest for your soul in these pages.

**My Prayer:** Lord, help me remember to search for Your way and to remember that each day You have surprises waiting for me around the corner. Amen.

**Extra Steps:** "This is what the Lord says: stand at the crossroads and look; ask for the ancient paths, ask where the good way is, and walk in it, and you will find rest for your souls". Jeremiah 6:16

# 2

## Home is Where...

So we are home again! Every year I anticipate coming home. We have spent our winters in Florida for several years, and I enjoy that time and the friends we have there; however, my home is here in Edgar County, Illinois.

Home is where the grass is greener, the leaves on the trees are bigger, the sound of the birds chirping in my back yard is louder, the flowers are brighter and most of all my memories are here. Home is where the familiar face greets you at the Post Office, the driver meeting you at the stop sign waves in recognition, and the old friend (and I mean old) greets you at church with a warm smile and a "welcome home."

Home is where I hear the drone of the tractor and the smell of the fresh black dirt as it is turned for planting. Home is where my great-granddaughter hugs me and my grandson calls to tell us "come by for mushrooms." No need to explain who I am, who my children are, what I did before retirement or what I do for fun. My history is here. I am home!

As I write this, I am reminded of the song called "Going Home" by B.J. Thomas, which starts with these lyrics…

> "They say that heaven's pretty,
> and living here is too.
> But if they said
> that I would have to choose between the two.
> I'd go home, going home, where I belong."[1]

During my walk this morning, I reminded myself that even though I am glad to be here, this is not really my home. As the song continues, "I'm just passing through."

**My Prayer:** Thank You for my home here, but even more for the promise I have for a heavenly home just around the corner. Amen.

**Extra Steps:** "For we know that if the earthly tent we live in is destroyed, we have a building from God, an eternal house in heaven, not built by human hands". Corinthians 5:1

# 3

# Prepared

I began to plan my day as I turned down Wood Street and started home. Preparation and planning are part of my personality. I don't really like to do things on the spur of the moment. When my husband suggests, "Oh, let's just drive and see what happens," I do not get excited.

I want to know what's going to happen, where I am going and if I have a place to stay when I get there. I am much more content if I know the road we are going to travel. The more prepared I am the happier I am.

So when Jesus tells me to quit worrying because He is preparing a place for me, and that He is going to come back and get me, I feel content and at peace. It becomes a truly personal thing. He is getting my room ready; He knows where I am going to stay; He has told me the way. It's better than a GPS! Jesus is taking care of my journey and is preparing my room.

The best part is that he is expecting me. He's there now waiting for me. I don't have to be troubled and make all the plans and take care of all the details–Jesus is doing that. All I have to do is travel the road of life with trust because

He is the way and my place is ready and waiting. What a tremendous blessing! I can travel this journey of life with peace because I know the plan.

**My Prayer:** Thank You for going ahead and leaving a plan for me to travel on the journey of life. Help me to follow Your plan so I will reach the destination You have already prepared for me. Amen.

**Extra Steps:** "Do not let your hearts be troubled. Trust in God; trust also in me. In my Father's house are many rooms; if it were not so, I would have told you. I am going there to prepare a place for you. And if I go and prepare a place for you, I will come back and take you to be with me that you also may be where I am. John 14:1-3

**Extra Steps:** "For I know the plans I have for you," declares the LORD, "plans to prosper you and not to harm you, plans to give you hope and a future." Jeremiah 29:11

### Sample 10-Week Walking Plan

| Week | 1 | 2 | 3 | 4 | 5 | 6 | 7 | 8 | 9 | 10 |
|---|---|---|---|---|---|---|---|---|---|---|
| # of minutes | 10 | 10 | 15 | 18 | 20 | 20 | 25 | 30 | 32 | 35 |
| Walks per Week | 2 | 3 | 3 | 3 | 3-4 | 4 | 4 | 4 | 4 | 4 |

**Taken from U.S. Dept. of Veteran Affairs website)

# 4

## Different Changes

Perhaps it is the spring rains, but as I walk this morning bright green seems to surround me. Crossing the edge of the schoolyard, I notice large patches of bright yellow dandelions spread out in the green grass. I step closer and glimpse little purple violets hidden in the patches of yellow. My steps leave footprints indented in the soft earth, and the clouds overhead predict more rain.

It seems it has rained almost every day since we arrived home. But it is spring in Illinois, and I am home. And for that I am always thankful. I appreciate Florida in the winter, but Edgar County will always be home.

Change has welcomed us back. Wal-Mart's aisles are in different order; the big water tank behind our house seems almost finished; the gas tanks at Ray's station are vanishing; some buildings are gone. As always, the biggest change is the loss of familiar faces no longer here to greet us. Sickness and accidents have taken the life of friends and family. We contend with this each year. And yet the babies have grown and new ones are expected. The normal changes of life continue.

No matter how things change, they somehow stay the

same. Vacation Bible School time is here again at Bell Ridge (our local congregation). More than seventy children fill the building with songs of joy, cheers of encouragement, and cries of recognition as they greet teachers and friends.

Bible School, too, has changed. It is in the morning this year. All of the songs and announcements are in the computer and are shown as a video on the big screen. A clever young teenager leads the singing. Young teenagers are everywhere as helpers. No longer are home-made cookies and Kool-Aid the refreshments. Now healthy foods which relate to the lesson are the fare of the day. Men portraying Bible characters, acting in the skits, and directing the play time is certainly different than the all-women staff we once had. Some of these changes I like, and some I'm not sure about. However, I have walked through many years of Bible School.

John F. Kennedy once said, "The one unchangeable certainty is that nothing is certain or unchangeable." In the earthly realm I agree that nothing is certain; however, the one certainty in life that keeps all of life's changes minor is the Word of God. God's promises in His Word never change.

In Malachi 3:6 (the last book of the Old Testament) Malachi writes, "For I the Lord do not change…" Paul wrote to the Romans Christians that "Jesus Christ is the same yesterday, today and forever." (Hebrews 13:8). The promise I lean upon is Jesus' promise right before he ascended to be with His father, "I will be with you always even unto the end of the world" (Matthew 28:20). Always and unchanging are common thoughts in God's Word.

Even when some changes are difficult, I can accept, appreciate and live with them in this secular environment because I have the promise of an ageless, unchanging, beautiful life in heaven.

**My Prayer:** Lord, let me be gracious and loving to accept the changes around me. Help me to remember that these earthly happenings are only the preface to an unchanging, eternal life with You. Amen.

**Extra Steps:** "Jesus Christ is the same yesterday, today and forever." Hebrews 13:8

## SEASONAL WALKING SAFETY TIPS

WINTER WALKING:
- Dress in layers
- Remember hat and gloves
- Wear shoes which will grip snow and ice
- Walk with hands out of pockets for better balance

SPRING WALKING:
- Check weather /be prepared for rain

SUMMER WALKING:
- Drink water before walking/carry extra water
- Recognize signs of heat sickness

FALL WALKING:
- Layer clothing for both warm and cold temperatures
- A hat, light jacket and/or umbrella are good to carry

Photo Credit: Ruth E. Newhart

# 5

# Storm Watch

When I started my walk, the sky was an early morning blue and the sun in the east was beginning to turn orange. Everything around was still a bit hazy, but the birds were singing. I could hear the traffic on Route 150, as the world woke up to another work day.

I decided to walk up to Schwartz Park again this morning, so I started through the school yard and over to the black top road behind the school. A few geese had already found the early morning worms in the dirt around the track. They hardly noticed me. Some city workers were checking the new water facility as they do every morning.

At this point in my walking I usually wait for the school buses to leave, but summer break has started so the long row of buses sat unusually quiet waiting for repairs and maintenance to begin. As I turned at the corner onto Wood Street, I rejoiced in the sun and the beautiful day that stretched ahead.

Suddenly, a distant rumble, a dark cloud and a breath of heavy wind warned me of an approaching storm. I quickly turned for home as I knew our area was going to get another squall. They come up so quickly that we hardly have time to find shelter, shut the windows, or take the wash from the line. I shut the windows on the van and put my sheets in the washer before I started walking so I hurried home to safety.

These summer storms have been coming so suddenly that we have little time to prepare for them. Yesterday afternoon when I went into the Walmart, the sun was shining brightly, and when I started to leave sheets of rain were blowing across the parking lot, and water was running in the streets. My umbrella was in my van, of course.

It occurs to me that the storms of life are much the same. Our lives are full of happiness, job is good, kids are healthy, and all is well in our world. Then, without warning the storm hits. Our breadwinner gets laid off without notice; a loved one receives a serious diagnosis; the bills begin to stack up.

Often we have prepared, but sometimes we find that "we have left the umbrella in the van." We are not prepared for the downpour of trouble we are facing. It's then I turn to God and yell "Help!" As I have walked through the storms of life, I have found praying and reading His Word have been an "umbrella", but have also prepared me a bit more for the next time… and there is always a next time.

**My Prayer:** Help me to remain close to You and Your people Lord. May I have your strength through prayer to overcome the storms of life. Help me to be an example to those around me when the storms strike that they might find comfort in my strength. Amen.

**Extra Steps:** "But in your hearts revere Christ as Lord. Always be prepared to give an answer to everyone who asks you to give the reason for the hope that you have. But do this with gentleness and respect." 1 Peter 3:15

# 6

# Beautiful Weeds

Rainy, spring weather has caused much concern for the farmer, but the area roadsides and homesteads reflect myriad colors of green and yellow. It is the yellow I find so interesting Acre after acre covered with the golden yellow "flower." In some places, as much as an 80-acre field is covered with the sunshine yellow plant.

My husband tells me they are weeds, a mustard plant, rocket weed or parsnips. I can hardly believe that something so beautiful could be a weed. I had commented previously about the beauty in the fields, and it was then he indicated in his farmer voice that the "beautiful flower" was nothing but a weed. Apparently, prior preparation of the ground or applying a spray in the fall can deter growth of the flowers I find so beautiful. Beautiful, but it's a weed. Rather interesting isn't it?

I thought about that as I walked this morning when I noticed a few stems in one of the empty fields. Rather like sin isn't it? Sin often looks so beautiful. How could there be harm in something that is so much fun? How could God not want us to feel good about ourselves all the time? Surely God does not mean this lovely way of living is sinful? And perhaps

13

it isn't, many beautiful things of the life are God-given and blessed, but like the beauty of the yellow field, some things in life when you look at them closely are weeds.

Somewhat like the mustard weed, no matter what we call it, a weed is a weed and sin is sin. Just as spraying and working the ground before spring blooming can put off the growth of the yellow weed, so preparation before we are tempted to sin can also keep us from surrendering to our sinful desires.

Knowing verses that answer our specific temptations is good early preparation. I like pretty clothes—nothing sinful about that unless it becomes all-important in my life. God's Word tells me in Matthew that I need not worry about what I am going to wear. God will take care of it. I have this verse memorized.

Many people let the acquisition of material possessions become the guiding factor in life. God's Word does not indicate that we are not to have material possessions. If the acquisition of "things" has become our goal, then we need to remember God's admonition. "Seek ye first the kingdom of God and His righteousness and all these things will be added unto you" (Matthew 6:33).

Prayer is also good preparation against the lovely weed of sin. A solid prayer life is necessary if we are to continue to live in a way that is pleasing to God. He tells us to "Pray without ceasing" (1 Thessalonians 5:17). If we have prepared our lives by praying and asking for strength, we find ourselves much better prepared for the struggles that face us each day.

Will we sin? Of course, but just as farmers recognize that the beautiful yellow weed is a weed, we too need to recognize sin even when it is so appealing. Recognition and preparation will not totally destroy the growth of a few yellow weeds and neither will they totally wipe sin from our life, but they are a process of prevention.

**My Prayer:** Lord, I want to be able to recognize that sin can often appear to be a beautiful happening. Help me prepare ahead of time to fight the sin that will grow in my life if I am not prepared. Amen.

**Extra Steps:** "If anyone, then, knows the good they ought to do and doesn't do it, it is  sin for them." James 4:17

## Six Benefits to Get up and Walk

- Regular walking burns calories

- Half of the body's muscles are designed for walking/ natural movement

- Regular brisk walking has many health benefits

- Brisk walking is an aerobic activity that benefits the heart and lungs

- Regular walking refreshes mind, reduces fatigue and improves sleep

- Walking can be great time to socialize with family and friends

# 7

# My Plans

I know God chuckles at our feeble efforts to make plans. We are so intent on what we feel is best that we forget to wait on the Lord. "But they that wait upon the Lord shall renew their strength; they shall mount up with wings as eagles; they shall run, and not be weary; and they shall walk, and not faint" (Isaiah 40:30-31). God tells us He knows the plans He has for us— "plans to prosper us, not to harm us" (Jeremiah 29:11).

We know these things. We quote these verses. Yet, we often make our decisions without waiting for God. Then something happens or several somethings, and we realize that God is God and we are not.

In the past few months, I decided that perhaps writing was not the way God wanted to use me. I no longer felt He had something to say through me. I really quit trying to do much with the written word beyond the blog entry for my Kindred Heart writing group and once in a six-week period I had written a short devotion for the group. My www.clellascorner.blogspot.com was almost obsolete and no submissions found their way to my editors' desk. No new pages were produced for my now old idea about spices.

16

Excuse after excuse flowed. I had decided I was done writing. After all, I am getting older (notice I did not say old, just older.) I was not too sad with this idea. Writing takes time and is hard work. I was enjoying my days of leisure.

But this tiny guilt feeling kept nudging when I walked, when I wasn't playing, when I read my devotions. So I prayed "God what do you want me to do now? I am ready to do something else for you." Notice I am telling God I want to do something besides write. In fact, I have a few ideas, and I shared them with Him.

As I walked this morning, I said, "Good morning." to the lady walking toward me. She responded, "Oh I'm so glad I met you. I'm reading your book and I just love it." "Oh?" The surprise must have been evident. "My friend loaned it to me and now my husband and I are both reading it. Can I buy two? I want one for myself and one as a gift for a friend." She came by my home later and purchased the books.

While she was there, another friend asked to buy a book for her friend. It has been quite a while since I have personally sold any books, and now I have sold three within an hour. Later the same day, my phone rang. A friend I had not heard from since Christmas calling to visit, to check on us and to ask why I wasn't posting on my blog. I really had no answer. "Well, I'll pray about it." she commented as we said our good-byes.

All in the same day God seems to be telling me "He knows the plans He has for me. His plan is the same as it has always been. He wants me to write. And so I will wait upon the Lord, and I will write, and my strength will be renewed and I will walk and not grow faint.

**My Prayer:** Lord, I need to be reminded that You have my life in Your hands. Give me the wisdom to pay attention to your heeding. Help me to use the gifts You have given me Amen.

**Extra Steps:** "For I know the plans I have for you," declares the Lord, "plans to prosper you and not to harm you, plans to give you hope and a future." Jeremiah 29:11

### SAFETY RULES

BE AWARE. CROSS WITH CARE
- Make eye contact with drivers turning right before stepping into crosswalk. Don't assume that because the car in lane closest to you has stopped that other cars will stop too.

DON'T BE DEAD RIGHT
- Pedestrians do have the right of way at marked and unmarked crosswalk; but some drivers might not know the rule or follow it. Being right will not keep you from being hit.

DISTRACTED WALKING IS DEADLY
- Unplug headphones when crossing the street
- Hang up your cell phone until you are out of intersection
- Texting must wait
- Look up!! Make eye contact if at all possible.

Courtesy of the "Speed and Pedestrian Safety Management on North Virginia and Sierra Streets project by the Davidson Academy Of Nevada and UNR Police Services

# 8

# Making Jesus Attractive

So many prayers as I walk. I pray for a young person that he might accept Christ. I pray for a family that is in strife. I feel heartache and despair in the world. I remind myself that God is in control, and I am not. My job is to make His Son attractive to those I meet when I turn each corner in my walk through life.

Today I will start a study of Philippians with a group of women. Starting a new Bible study is rather like turning the corner when you are walking a familiar path. The path is the same one you have walked previously, but when you turn the corner you often see something you have missed before.

One day I noticed a picnic table in a wooded area I walk by each day. Of course it has been there all the time because I walk the same route, but I just haven't noticed it before. Well, that happened to me today in my Bible study.

I turned the page this morning and found a truth—not a new truth, but new to me. We are reading (Philippians 1:7-11). As I read this passage, it became clear to me that the real truth in today's reading was the verse that reads "Live a lover's life, circumspect and exemplary, a life Jesus will be proud of: bountiful in fruits from the soul, making Jesus

Christ attractive to all, getting everyone involved in the glory and praise of God." (Philippians 1:10-11 The Message)[2]

And there is my thought for the day—"making Jesus Christ attractive to all" Isn't that an exemplary thought? For several weeks now, I have been dwelling on this idea of how our everyday living attracts or repels the people we come in contact with. I think of the clerks in the store, the waitress in the restaurant, the lady who delivers my paper or the child who sees me at Wal-Mart.

Do I reflect Christ to them? Do I make Jesus attractive? Do they think "whatever it is that woman has in her life, I want it? I want that kind of joy, that kind of peace, that kind of happiness in my life." Shouldn't it be our goal as we walk through this life to make Jesus attractive? This is not always easy in today's society, but it is a goal that we need to move toward. Let those of us who are walking with the Son attempt to make Jesus attractive in the our society.

**My Prayer:** Help people see the love of Jesus when they watch my actions. May they feel the love of Christ when they are in my presence. Make my life a life that makes Jesus attractive to those around me. Amen.

**Extra Steps:** "Finally, brothers and sisters, whatever is true, whatever is noble, whatever is right, whatever is pure, whatever is lovely, whatever is admirable—if anything is excellent or praiseworthy—think about such things. Whatever you have learned or received or heard from me, or seen in me—put it into practice…" Philippians 4:8-9

# 9

# Trust

When I walk, I often pray for my family. My great-granddaughters have brought me much joy. I frequently smile as I remember their sweet hugs and humorous comments. The words of a child are often so true. Jesus told us to have the attitude of a little child. Today, I thought about my latest encounter with Pailynne, our five year-old.

Her bright eyes follow my every move. Earlier she had asked to watch me "fix my face", and now the process is beginning. (and it is a process) As she perches on the bathroom vanity, she scoots her little body across the counter top and scrunches her sweet five-year-old face in the mirror.

I apply my foundation and dot her waiting face with two small dots. I brush on my "bare essentials" make-up and run the brush across the freckles on her nose. We share the blush and then the powder. All is well until I pick up the eye-lash curler, "Do it to me Grandma, do it to me", and she bats her eyes and tilts her head in imitation of my head tilting.

"Oh honey, we can't share this. I'm afraid I'll hurt you."

"But you wouldn't hurt me. You're my Grandma."

21

The innocence and trust of my great-granddaughter's remark touched me, and I recalled it often in the next few days. While walking this morning, I smiled and thought again of her absolute trust that I wouldn't hurt her because I was her Grandma.

"Trust in the Lord with all your heart and lean not on your own understanding." came to mind. Sometimes it is hard for me to understand why God's plan is not what I want. I remind myself that this Scripture is for me. I sometimes question God's answers to my requests, especially if He seems to be answering "No."

Each time I begin to doubt I need to have the trusting faith of a child. I want to trust His Word just as Pailynne believes in me. May I respond as she did. "You won't hurt me...you're my Lord."

**My Prayer:** Give me faith to trust You, Lord. I want to understand that the plans You have for me are for my benefit. Thank You for Pailynne in my life. May she always be able to trust me with such a child-like faith. Amen.

**Extra Steps:** "It (*love*) always protects, always trusts, always hopes, always perseveres."
1 Corinthians 13:7

# 10

# Walk the Talk

It matters not if I am in my Illinois home or our place in sunny Florida. They are everywhere. Many more than I would have thought. This morning, in the area surrounding my neighborhood, I counted eight. I know others were there earlier, and many more emerge during the cooler evening hours. Not the geese I wrote about another time, but the walkers. I am always surprised by the number of people who walk as a part of their daily exercise regimen.

Walking for exercise and meditation seems to be for all ages, sizes, and nationalities. Magazine covers, book stores and videos are filled with stories of the rewards of a personal walking program. Because I am a walker, I often reach for the magazine with "New Personal Walking Program" as its latest promise. Or the latest edition of Family Circle© that has emblazoned "WALK OFF MORE WEIGHT" in bright orange letters on the cover. Walking books are a part of my personal library, and every famous star seems to have an exercise or walking video available for $19.95.

All are filled with good advice and excellent illustrations, but reading and watching give me little result. I read them all (well not all, but probably too many).

Through experience I have discovered that reading the article or watching the video does very little except waste my time. I have "book learning" about walking, but if I don't walk, my knowledge does me no good. Talking the walk doesn't make me a walker.

Isn't it the same with those of us who call ourselves Christians? In today's society many are identifying with the name of Christian, but reading the Book and watching the preacher do not make us Christians any more than reading the article in the magazine and watching the video makes me a walker. I tell people I walk, but if I wear out after walking a block, I surely haven't done much more than read the instructions. I haven't been practicing enough.

I claim the name of Christian, but 'if I have not love, I am as a clanging cymbal" only good for noise" (1Corinthians 13:1). I attend the services of the local congregation on Sunday, sing, pray, and greet my fellow Christians. If on Monday my tongue is cutting and cursing those same people, I am only reading the Scripture not practicing what I have read. I have knowledge, but no action. James says "To know to do good and not to do it is as sin" (James 4:17).

God's Word tells us that even Satan knows the Scripture. Knowing and doing are different parts of the Christian walk. Of course, we need to know God's Word, but until we start walking it, His Word is useless. As reading the books and magazines does nothing for my physical body, reading and studying do little for my spiritual well-being. I must walk the walk. I encourage you to walk spiritually as well as physically.

**My Prayer:** Help me to walk on the path that You have for me. May I be an example to those around me that I am "practicing what I preach". Amen.

**Extra Steps:** "If I speak in the tongues of men or of angels, but do not have love, I am only a resounding gong or a clanging cymbal." 1 Corinthians 13:1

**Extra Steps:** "not giving up meeting together, as some are in the habit of doing, but encouraging one another—and all the more as you see the Day approaching." Hebrews 10:25

## Walking Mistakes

- Over Striding
- Wrong Shoes
- Flapping or slapping feet
- Not using arms
- Swinging arms across the body
- Head down
- Leaning (forward, back, swaying)
- Wrong clothes
- Not drinking enough
- Overtraining (even God rested)

Courtesy of WendyBaumgardner (Guide toWalking,www.walking.about.com)

# 11

# Price of Freedom

Awooden Uncle Sam waves an American flag as he guards the corner of my neighbor's lawn. Each corner I turn I see small symbols of America. Flags, bunting and windsocks flutter in the subtle breeze. The clang of a barbeque grill in a local back yard puts a feeding squirrel up the nearest tree.

Music floats from the sound system of a teenager's vehicle as it stops at the four-way intersection. Childish laughter from the children down the street echoes above the edges of their newly installed pool and hovers on the surface of the neighborhood. Serene, soothing sounds of America as it prepares for another summer celebration.

July 4th is fast approaching. Here in this Edgar County, Illinois town (population 10,000) tradition is strong. Food, flags, fun and fireworks are the order of the day. First the parade, and then we flock with family and friends to the local parks for fellowship with young and old.

A great-grandmother rocks the newest baby in her arms as she applauds her grandson's solo in the city band concert. Horseshoes clang against the iron stake. Mothers scold and fathers chat. Children chase in among the adults

27

begging for one more cotton candy, one more goofy-golf game, one more ride in the paddle boats.

The day builds as the darkness approaches. Blankets and lawn chairs start spotting the grass like beacons for the children in the early twilight. A low murmur of expectation, crying babies, and muttering parents mingles with the high pitched whine of tired children. Red stars burst on the night sky and the fireworks begin. Moans of appreciation explode from the crowd, and another 4th of July is celebrated in my home town.

Edgar County is a small spot in the American countryside, but we understand, perhaps more than some small towns, the price for freedom. Recent deaths of five of our local National Guard soldiers in Iraq gives a bittersweet gratefulness to our heritage. Beneath the surface of every Fourth of July celebration is our first-hand knowledge of the sacrifice and sadness that has made it possible. We see the veteran's memorial on our town square and are aware of those who have given. No matter our faith, we surely must be thankful for that heritage we really don't deserve.

**My Prayer:** Join me in prayer for those families who have given so much, and for those who are still giving that we can walk and pray and worship with our family. Thank them and God that we can be a part of America. With all its faults, people are still struggling and giving their lives that we can maintain this freedom and I am personally thankful for that effort. May God truly bless us all. Amen.

**Extra Steps:** "I urge then, first of all, that requests, prayers, intercession and thanksgiving be made for everyone, for kings and all those in authority, that we may live peaceful and quiet lives in all godliness and holiness. This is good and pleases God our Savior." 1 Timothy 2:2-6

# 12

# Never Say Amen

During my Monday morning walks I often consider the sermon I heard on Sunday. Yesterday's sermon was referenced in Ecclesiastes, and I began to explore my feelings about what I heard.

Isn't it interesting that the preacher's statement in Ecclesiastes "there is nothing new under the sun" is so true? Recently, I heard a young woman exclaim as we discussed prayer, "I never say Amen." I have been rethinking her comment. It really is the same thought as "Pray without ceasing" (1 Thessalonians 5:17).

The longer I live the more I pray. It would seem a person would get better at praying as time goes on, but in my case I realize each day how much I need God's help for everything I do. The "pray without ceasing" admonition has become my motto.

God is so good to me that I must spend so much time thanking Him for the blessings of the day. Then someone gets sick, and I must go to Him for peace and healing. Before I realize it, someone in the church is in trouble spiritually, physically or mentally, and I need to talk to God on their behalf. He is the only one who can heal.

29

So the hours go by and the day is over, and it is time for rest, and he gives it to me every night. My mother once had a quote beside her bed that read "give your cares to God before you sleep because He is going to be up anyway" I try to do that and I usually sleep well.

I try to keep my lines to God open by continuous prayer. I can see His hand in all my life from the smallest of details to the overall story of the seventy-nine years I have lived. I would encourage you to go each day to His Word and then to prayer.

**My Prayer:** My prayer for today is that you will be uplifted and encouraged to talk to God and never say, Amen.

**Extra Steps:** "What has been will be again, what has been done will be done again; there is nothing new under the sun." Ecclesiastes 1:9

**Extra Steps:** "Be joyful in hope, patient in affliction, faithful in prayer." Romans 12:12

### Prayer Tips

- Pray for safety before you start

- Pray for the people you meet

- Pray for the homes you go by

# 13

## Anticipation

We start another trip today. I am excited and a bit apprehensive. Each time we make plans to travel I feel this way and this morning is no exception. For the first time, I personally made all of the plans down to the last detail. I enjoy the planning, packing and researching. Anticipation is part of the journey.

We made plans for our flight and our transfer to the ship. We have read and studied about the areas we will be visiting. The areas are all new to us, and we want to enjoy and learn all we can while we are in each location.

Some of our Florida friends live in Halifax and we are meeting them for lunch and a tour of their city. They have spread the word to other friends in the area, and plans have been made for us to share some time with all of them. What fun that will be! My plans are finished now. We will leave this afternoon. I review the plans one more time. Have I done all I could do to get ready?

I return from walking and drop into the lawn chair. As I rest and consider our trip, I am reminded that someday I will take another trip. I have made the plans and done all I know to prepare for the journey.

As I plan for this future time, I anticipate the friends I will meet at my destination. I expect they have shared with mutual friends that I am coming. I enjoy the planning, the preparing and the studying before I go, but the best part is the anticipation. I ask myself often, "Have I done all I could to get ready?"

And just as our earthly trip will be better than we anticipated, so my heavenly destination will be so much better than my anticipation. Are you anticipating this heavenly journey?  Have you done all you can to get ready?

**My Prayer:** Lord, I am excited about my heavenly journey. Thank You for Your Word describing my heavenly destination and the plans I need to make to get there. May I be ready for the journey.  Amen.

**Extra Steps:** "But our citizenship is in heaven, and from it we await a Savior, the Lord Jesus Christ, who will transform our lowly body to be like his glorious body, by the power that enables him even to subject all things to himself." Philippians 3:20- 21

**Extra Steps:** "He will wipe away every tear from their eyes, and death shall be no more, neither shall there be mourning, nor crying, nor pain anymore, for the former things have passed away power that enables him even to subject all things to himself." Revelations 21:4

# 14

# Proud Memory

This morning as I scurried around to finish my chores before walking, I thought of our experience in the Boston airport as we returned from our trip up the eastern Atlantic seaboard. Perhaps since there is so much garbage about our country in the news right now, this memory might take you around the corner into a better day.

*Diary Entry.    Saturday morning,   9/22/12    3:45 a.m.*

I woke up startled; feeling alarmed. We had not received our morning wake up call. We had fifteen minutes to catch the shuttle to the airport. We arrived in good time and made our way to the airport McDonald's for a sausage and egg biscuit. While we were eating, several young men in military fatigues sat near us also enjoying their breakfast.

At our 7:00 a.m. boarding time, the Delta agent indicated that all military could board first, and surprisingly the same young military men hustled into the tunnel toward the plane. Our flight was uneventful and while in flight I inquired where they were headed.  Smiling big, he responded, "We're coming home Ma'am. We've been gone for a year."

When we arrived at the Boston airport, we exited the plane right behind these soldiers. Walking into the terminal, we spotted a group of young women and children huddled together in a band of excitement. Just as we passed them a little girl darted by me and ran to the arms of one of the young men. Tears began to flow. We turned to watch the reunion and my heart overflowed with pride as the crowd in the terminal began a round of applause that grew and echoed in the Boston airport. I was proud to be an American. What a wonderful memory for the start of our journey.

**My Prayer:** Thank you, Lord, that I have been blessed to be a citizen of this country. Help me to remember the men and women who are away from their loved ones so that I might be so free to move from state to state without guns and guards. Amen.

**Extra Steps:** Give thanks in all circumstances; for this is God's will for you in Christ Jesus. 1 Thessalonians 5:18

"...It is a proud privilege to be a soldier – a good soldier ... [with] discipline, self-respect, pride in his unit and his country, a high sense of duty and obligation to comrades and to his superiors, and a self-confidence born of demonstrated ability."
—George S. Patton Jr.

# 15

## My Pleasure or His

I have been reading Rick Warren's *The Purpose Driven Life.* He writes that our focus should not be "How much pleasure am I getting out of life?" but rather, "How much pleasure is God getting out of my life?"[3]

How much pleasure is God getting out of my life? I certainly get pleasure from my life. I live in America. My husband, my children and my grandchildren are healthy, both spiritually and physically. We go, we do, we enjoy so many things. Perhaps, self-examination time is here. Is my life pleasurable to God? I ask myself what things pleasure me that our children do? The same things it seems would please God our Father.

I am pleased when our children obey. Now that they are older, I find great joy when they reflect the things we have taught them. It delights me when I witness our adult children teaching their children the things they have learned from us.

God may also be pleased when I teach his children the truths I have learned from his Word that they too might mature as Christians. Peter tells us we should "grow up" (1

35

Peter 2:2). Perhaps not as much as God might want, but just as I can see physical and spiritual maturity happen in our earthly children, He can see the minute details of growth in my life. I do hope He is satisfied.

I am pleased when our children have more than a "hello/goodbye" conversation with us. Our child's problems and griefs are always important to us, but how gratifying it is when a child (particularly an adult child) shares a dream with us. My daily prayers to God are filled with problems and requests. God is probably elated when I stop to share my dreams with Him.

I am pleased when our children show love and loyalty to one another and to the rest of the family. Because I have been "adopted" into the family of God, I need to show my loyalty to that family. My fellow Christians are my brothers and sisters, and my tongue should only praise and encourage them. How quickly I sometimes find fault with a brother in Christ. I pray this might change so that God might find more pleasure in this aspect of my daily living.

I am pleased when our children show appreciation for what we have done for them; not because they have to, but because they are truly appreciative. I don't say thank you enough to my earthly parent or to my God.

I turn the corner and start towards home as I finish this walk of self-examination. I remind myself again that our life here on earth is not really for our pleasure but for His.

**My Prayer:** All that I am and all that I have is from You, Oh Lord. The song of the bird mingles with the song of my child. Thank You God. The blue of the sky reflects in the summer pool full of laughing children. Thank You God. The love of my husband exemplifies Christ's love for me. Thank You God. My eternal thanks to You for the pleasure our children bring to my life. An infinite stream of my "thanks" should be flooding the ears of God. I pray that as Your child I fill You with much pleasure also.  Amen.

**Extra Steps:** "Therefore, rid yourselves of all malice and all deceit, hypocrisy, envy, and slander of every kind.  Like newborn babies, crave pure spiritual milk, so that by it you may grow up in your salvation, now that you have tasted that the Lord is good." 1 Peter 2:1-3

"Above all, do not lose your desire to walk: every day I walk myself into a state of well-being and walk away from every illness; I have walked myself into my best thoughts and I know of no thought so burdensome that one cannot walk away from it."
— Søren Kierkegaard

# 16

## County Fair Time

It's fair time! As I walked along Wood Street two vehicles pulling livestock trailers passed me, and I thought about the upcoming fair week. The excitement and fun of the fair began a couple of weeks ago when we attended the box seat auction. It was then I began to reminisce and anticipate the celebration of the 150th year of the Edgar County Fair.

Anticipation of the Fair was a part of my growing up years. As a small child, I would stand in front of the smeared glass pane of the cotton candy booth as the lady magically spun the beautiful pink sugar onto the paper cone. Now it comes in plastic bags. Where is the magic in that?) And then, the merry-go-round music would start, and I clutched my mother's hand waiting for my turn to mount the beautiful black pony. I remember watching the little ducks float by and grabbing the one you knew had the winning number for the teddy bear.

In my young teenage years, the 4-H fair was the highlight of the summer. Not only the cooking and sewing projects or the excitement of showing my Herford calf, but walking the carnival with my friends. How many trips did we make up and down the carnival route? The giggling girls in one group and the loud, obnoxious boys following. I'm not sure that has changed.

As a young bride in the summer of 1955, I attended the horse races with my in-laws. They loved the county fairs. My soldier husband was not around that summer, and I learned about harness racing from Dad Camp at the County Fair.

And in a few years, our children began the fair anticipation/participation cycle. History repeating itself as we did the dog obedience class at the 4-H fair, and I know our teenage children walked the carnival.

Soon, (and it seems very soon) our grandchildren were toddlers. The Edgar County Fair was the place for their first Carousel ride, their first Ferris Wheel ride as they hold hands to keep Grandma from being scared, and the journey down the big slide in Dad's lap. Those toddlers slid right into teenagers walking the carnival as I had fifty years before.

As Edgar County celebrates its 150th year, I am anticipating participating with our great-granddaughter as I watch her ride the Merry-Go Round, or eat a corn dog or wipe some cotton candy off her sticky face.

The joy is in the anticipation and then the participation. I have been thinking about how that is also true of our Christian faith. When we participate in the fellowship, in the work, in the meeting together we then turn the corner and experience the joy and excitement of being a part of the family of God. As we participate in the things of God, we anticipate not only our time together here on earth, but perhaps also we can anticipate eternity. We don't anticipate if we don't participate whether it's the celebration of the Fair or the celebration of eternity.

**My Prayer:** I am anticipating eternity Lord. Please, help me prepare each day for the time when I can be with You in Heaven. I want to be ready. Amen.

**Extra Steps**: "He has made everything beautiful in its time. He has also set eternity in the human heart; yet no one can fathom what God has done from beginning to end." Ecclesiastes 3:11

**Extra Steps:** For the creation eagerly awaits with anticipation for God's sons to be revealed." Romans 8:19

## Walking Benefits

- Your mood will improve

- Your creative juices will start flowing.

- You'll slash your risk of chronic disease.

- You'll keep your legs looking great.

- Your jeans will get a little loose

# 17

## Off Balance

I am off balance. Walking a straight line today would be difficult if not impossible. If I lie down or stand up too fast the room moves, and instant nausea momentarily overwhelms me.

In the past, when I have experienced this condition, medications, slow movement and rest have always been the remedy. One does not function effectively when the world is tilted and the body is queasy.

The ups and downs of life can affect me spiritually just as a time of vertigo affects me physically. Life's traumatic events can cause our world to tilt and our spiritual life to become unsettled. We are still upright, but our decisions and reactions are not our normal Christian response to daily situations.

We are spiritually dizzy. We are frequently put off-balance by the major happenings of life—death, illness, accidents, job loss, economy. We become nauseous with worry and experience doubt and misgiving about God's care. Instead of restoring our balance by resting in God's promises, we turn our back and stumble away thinking to heal ourselves.

42

Even something as simple as not reading our Bible for a few days can throw us out of kilter. Our response to the people around us is out of balance. Anger quickly becomes a part of our day. Cross words, hateful remarks and sullen attitudes control our state of mind. I have found myself asking, "Now why did I say that?" I really didn't mean to act that way. I wish I could get out of this mood." A bit of rest and some time in God's Word often heal my mood and restore stability into my world.

Separating ourselves from our friends and the people who love us also causes us to become unbalanced spiritually. God tells us that as Christians we need to be with one another. When we neglect the "gathering of ourselves together," (Hebrews 10:25) we begin to think only of ourselves, our needs, our wants and our world.

We lose interest in neighbors and community. God created us to be a community of believers, and we walk best when we walk with others of like faith. We encourage one another, and in this encouragement we are able to find healthy spiritual balance.

Balance can be found in prayer. 1 Thessalonians 5:17 tells us to "pray without ceasing". The longer I live the more I pray. It would seem you would get better at it as time goes on, but in my case I realize each day how much I need God's help for anything I do. Days without talking with God are certainly unusual for me, but it does happen, and when it does I find my walk is difficult, and the path of life is full of bumps and curves. Many of the curves are those I have created in my off-balanced, lack of prayer walking. Letting God heal my daily situations and depending on Him to guide me keeps my way much straighter.

I am convinced this uneasy physical condition will pass if I maintain my regime of meclizine, slow motion and rest. Our spiritual unbalance may also pass if we read God's

Word, spend time with the community of believers and pray. Resting in God's promises is a sure cure for our spiritual imbalance.

**My Prayer:** God, don't let me become overbalanced spiritually. Help me to stay close to You so that I can continue to walk spiritually safe. And Lord, if it is your will, take away this physical unbalance that so often affects me. Amen.

**Extra Steps:** "not giving up meeting together, as some are in the habit of doing, but encouraging one another—and all the more as you see the Day approaching."
Hebrews 10:25

**Extra Steps:** "Do your best to present yourself to God as one approved, a worker who does not need to be ashamed and who correctly handles the word of truth."
2 Timothy 2:15

He who limps is still walking.

—Stanislaw J. Lec

# 18

## Encouragement

I walk with heavy heart. Members of our church family are angry with one another. I have experienced this several times in the congregation, but it always brings me to the Lord in prayer.

If we are to grow spiritually, we must love one another. We need to remember we are a family. My physical family is filled with adopted children. I have a niece, a nephew and two grandchildren who are an adopted part of our immediate family. They are our children and are treated no differently than birth children. We love each child in our family differently, but we love them all the same. To God, we are just like that. We are his adopted children, and we belong to the same family. Think about your church family. I encourage you to list at least five people who you feel truly are your brothers and sisters. Thank God for them and pray for them as you do your physical family.

So often in our church family, as in our physical family, people are hurt by careless or thoughtless actions and words. We need to be extra careful with our words and actions toward our church family. This week I encourage you to list three things you can do to keep members of your church family from being hurt either physically or spiritually.

Have you hurt someone in your church family unintentionally? Today is the day for forgiveness. Ask for forgiveness from the person and from God. Pray for the person and leave it at the foot of the cross. Burdens are not meant to be carried forever. Grudges, hurt feelings and unforgiving attitudes are not meant to be part of the family of God. When our relationship with God's children increases and becomes more loving, so does our love for God.

Pray that God will present you with the opportunity to encourage someone this week. Pray for your church family that you might walk around the corner with them on the road to spiritual growth. When we walk together the world may see Christ and it is then we walk in the abundant life Christ wants us to have.

My heart is lightened as I pray and make my list of those in my church family I can encourage this week.

**My Prayer:** Help me to encourage those I meet each day. Amen.

**Extra Steps:** "Encourage one another and build each other up, just as in fact you are doing." 1 Thessalonians 5:11

**Extra Steps:** "that is, that you and I may be mutually encouraged by each other's faith." Romans 1:12

# 19

## Change of Scenery

And the next day it rained! And the next- and the next. Green is the prevalent color of the landscape and colorful flowers are in abundance, but many of our farmers' crops are not what they should be in mid-July. It is easy to become discouraged. We get bogged down in our day to day living, particularly when each day is a rainy one. I function much better in sunshine.

The rainy weather becomes an excuse for not walking very far or very often. My walking route and my distance seem quite satisfactory to me. I walk the same streets, go the same direction and see the same scenery. Not that Briar Hill Road is bad scenery; just that it becomes tedious after several days. So, recently when the sun is shining, I have pushed myself a bit-going farther and walking a different route each day. As a result, I experience different scenery, enjoy life more and increase my physical strength.

In some ways, it is possible to do this same thing with our spiritual walking. We have all manner of excuses for not walking—rainy days, poor crops, bad health. Making a few changes brings us more joy and often more spiritual strength.

Bible reading is one area where I have attempted

47

to change my scenery and increase my distance. I read in the New Testament most of the time, and I particularly like the book of James. He speaks to me personally, and I am quite comfortable reading his letter and do it often. I don't particularly like to read in the Old Testament but am aware that much can be gained from reading the heroes of the Jewish Law. Lately, I have been reading and studying from some of the prophets, particularly Jeremiah, and if. I stay with it I will certainly become stronger and more knowledgeable. A bit of extra time and some unfamiliar scriptures can put new life into your Bible reading.

Prayer time can become rather humdrum also. We pray the same prayer, for the same people, in the same words at the same time. Even though God hears our prayers, they become hollow to us. Our prayers become rote recitation. Some people write their prayers. I have never done this, but I think it would certainly add meaning to my prayer time, and is something I am planning to try.

Also, I have been reading about "praying scripture." I have been studying this method and would challenge you to expand your prayer life in this way. Choose a section of scripture and insert your name or someone else's name where appropriate. Doing this may put new meaning into your prayer life.

Rather than use these rainy days as an excuse for dreary and hum-drum days, perhaps I can go farther and change my scenery both in my physical and my spiritual walking.

**My Prayer:** Keep me from being discouraged when life doesn't seem to be going as I would want it. Help me to prepare spiritually for those "rainy days" in life so that I can continue to walk as You would want me to walk. Amen.

**Extra Steps:** "I applied my mind to study and to explore by wisdom all that is done under the heavens. What a heavy burden God has laid on mankind!" Ecclesiastes 1:13

**Extra Steps:** "Do your best to present yourself to God as one approved, a worker who does not need to be ashamed and who correctly handles the word of truth." 2 Timothy 2:15

"Climb the mountains and get their good tidings. Nature's peace will flow into you as sunshine flows into trees, the storms their energy while cares will drop off like autumn leaves. As age comes on, one source of enjoyment after another is closed, but nature's sources never fail."
—John Muir

"How do geese know when to fly to the sun? Who tells them the seasons? How do we, humans know when it is time to move on? As with the migrant birds, so surely with us, there is a voice within if only we would listen to it, that tells us certainly when to go forth into the unknown."

—Elisabeth Kubler-Ross

# 20

## Flying High

I heard them even before I stepped out the door. The honking grated on my hearing aids somewhat like chalk on a board. Shading my eyes toward the sunrise, I could see the black V-formation gliding across the dawn of the October morning–geese flying south.

As I walked down the drive and started my morning trek, I listened to their honking and watched their progress across the sky. How do they know that flying in a V formation takes them 70 percent farther than flying alone?

As I head back home, I think about the geese and how they naturally fulfill the laws of nature. As they move toward their winter home in systematic V formation, I observe the command that all things be done in decency and in order illustrated against the rays of the morning sunrise.

Why do they fly far enough apart that they have the ability to watch each other and communicate about possible landing locations? The geese know instinctively how close they need to be in order to communicate. That strange grating honking noise warns their fellow flier about a safe landing place below or that one is in trouble. Communication between God's living creatures seems to be ingrained in animals as well as human beings.

When the lead bird gets tired it moves to the back and a new bird moves up to be the leader. What makes them know to do that? Why are geese so loyal that they usually mate for life? A family group stays together even within the flock.

If a flock member becomes injured or strays away, some of the family members will go down with the injured bird to keep it safe while it recuperates. When the bird is ready to fly again (or dies) will they leave, looking for a new group.

They instinctively know that they need one another to accomplish a goal. Letting the tired leader move to the back is not something they argue about. It is a natural change of leadership. Each member of the flock has its place and naturally realizes when it is time to move up so that the group might function more efficiently.

I notice one of the birds move out to pick up a straggling friend and guide it back into the formation, then continue flying along beside him. God's Word exemplified in the flight of the geese "if one falls down, his friend can help him up. But pity the man who falls and has no one to help him up" (Ecclesiastes 4:10). I walk along the edge of the water and watch as the beautiful birds rise again into the southern sky. Nature repeats itself year after year. It is an unending cycle.

And only His people can't seem to learn the pattern He has set for us. The birds do quite well. I pray that I might learn from the geese as I turn the corner to head towards home.

**My Prayer:** Help me to be aware when my friend has fallen. Make me loyal to my mate, my family and my friends. Give me the wisdom to recognize God's plan for me. Amen.

**Extra Steps:** "If either of them falls down, one can help the other up..."Ecclesiastes 4:10

### 10 Most Walkable Large Cities in United States
(walk score CBS based on 100 pt. scale)

| | |
|---|---|
| 1. New York City | 85 |
| 2. San Francisco | 84.9 |
| 3. Boston | 79.2 |
| 4. Chicago | 74.3 |
| 5. Philadelphia | 74.1 |
| 6. Seattle | 73.7 |
| 7. Washington D.C. | 73 |
| 8. Miami | 72.5 |
| 9. Minneapolis | 69.3 |
| 10. Oakland, CA | 68.2 |

# 21

## Check Your Closet

I walked last evening and then again this morning. I kept thinking about the words of the sermon I had heard on Sunday. I thought the message would fade in the Monday morning light as sermons so often do.

But here I am today, still hearing the minister's statement, "If you are called by My Name then look like one of My Kids. "The minister used Colossians 3:9-17 for the morning reading, and he paraphrased "Therefore, as God's chosen people, holy and dearly loved, clothe yourselves with."

*Clothe* is the word that caught me. The Message version is even more fascinating to me. "…dress in the wardrobe God picked out for you."

I must confess that clothes have always been important to me. I like pretty things more than I should and often spend too much time and money worrying about my clothes, and what I am going to wear. But God's message fell on my heart yesterday as I read from Colossians the apparel list that God has picked out for me.

**Compassion:** a deep felt emotion to see that a person's need is met

54

**Kindness:** taking our sincere, good intentions and making them happen

**Humility**: does not draw attention to self

**Gentleness**: responding to people in a calm and respectful manner

**Patience**: to be inconvenienced for a long period of time without complaining

**Forbearance:** Putting up with and accepting those things which rub us the wrong way about another-acceptance of the hurt

Sometimes I don't understand God's timing. I asked myself as I walked "How many times have you heard this scripture?" Why now does it make such an impact?

Perhaps He knows I need to dress my spirit more in His fashion. Perhaps because He knows me so well, He took this time and this messenger to remind me that my outward appearance only reflects my glory, but my spiritual clothing reflects His glory. I do want to be fashionable in God's attire and shine with His beauty.

I walk on in my sweatshirt and sweat pants and recognize that God wants me to look my physical best, but more than that He wants me to clothe myself with His righteousness.

**My Prayer:** Help me Lord to remember the apparel and the accessories for my spiritual life even as I am planning my physical wardrobe. Give me the wisdom to use both my physical and spiritual wardrobe for Your glory. In Jesus' name. Amen.

**Extra Steps**: "clothe yourselves with compassion, kindness, humility, gentleness and patience..." Colossians 3:12

# 22

## A Quiet Walk

A quiet walk this morning is exactly what I need. I love people, but sometimes a person needs to be alone. Maybe it is just in my life, but I don't think so. Quiet time seems to be something we all search for. I watch young mothers as they hurry from boss to babysitters, from babysitters to ball practice, from ball games to bedtime and wonder how they find time for the everyday tasks that must be accomplished.

And for the working grandmother it has become non-stop. Grandmothers, attempting to be all things to all people, flit from one grandchild to the next, go from one committee meeting, church meeting, lunch meeting or business meeting because *Society* has told us that good grandmothers can do it all. Grandmothers who don't have outside jobs frequently become the babysitter, and the merry-go round begins for them also.

Hovering like a dark cloud over all this to and fro is the latest DJ on the rock radio, the talk show on the television, the cell phone ringing in her purse, the television newscaster with the latest from Wall Street and the Schwann© man ringing the doorbell.

It isn't always the noise of the world that keeps us

from God, sometimes it is the noise within us. We don't stop long enough to let God speak to us. Rather we hurry from one thought to another, from one idea to another, from one comment to another without giving God any part of our mind. We seem to feel that we need to always be thinking, always planning, always doing something. God says, "Be still and know that I am God." (Psalms 46:10). We can hear God in many ways if we take the time.

Reading His Word and then considering what we have read is a good way to start. Praying and waiting for a response is also useful in hearing God. It is the waiting that is hard for me. I want Him to talk to me right now, and I want an answer, preferably my answer.

I can hear Him as I am walking this morning if only I pay attention. The geese are flying south; the leaves are turning from green to yellow; the harvest is happening; the air is getting cooler. All of this only demonstrates how consistent and faithful God is. The people and structures of our society may be changing and noisy, but if I slow down and listen I can recognize that God is still in charge of my life and is softly whispering "Be Still and Know that I AM."

We have allowed the world to take over our time. Perhaps we need to heed the words of the old hymn we sang on Sunday.

**My Prayer:** O Lord, May I take time to be holy. Amen.

## Extra Steps:

# 23

## Changes

Fields are beginning to be bare and geese honk as the shadow of their flight reflects on the water of the lake. Obviously the season is changing, and once again we will make the trip to our winter home in Florida. Even though I enjoy our home there, I find the change rather difficult at times. Perhaps it has something to do with age. I smile as I write that because I know it has much to do with age.

My mother lived for 92 years, and we often discussed the changes she had experienced in her life. As I walk this morning, many of the changes I have experienced in my lifetime come to mind.

I once read my favorite book, *Little Women*, by kerosene lamp; after electricity came into our home, I listened to The Lone Ranger on our very modern radio. I was in the third grade before our family had a bathroom and running water. Our ring on the party line telephone was two short and one long ring and the changes went on.

My high school graduation present was a modern electric typewriter; and later my children wore cloth diapers that I washed in a wringer washer and hung on the clothesline to dry in freezing winter weather. I taught myself about a computer on a new TRS-80 with DOS. I wore high-heeled shoes and skirts to teach school. Dial-up Internet was a miracle in Grandview, Illinois. And the changes went on.

Our son is now a grandfather. Our great-granddaughter celebrated her seventh birthday in September. She changes so quickly. What will she know in her lifetime? What changes will she experience as she walks into the future?

I can make few promises to her about her future. Changes will be many, but one promise I can make. "Jesus Christ is the same yesterday, today and forever" (Hebrews 13:8). If her faith is in Him as she walks through life, she can face any and all changes that come into her world. I walk on praying that she and all young children facing our changing world will realize this truth.

**My Prayer:** Help my family to realize as they continue this earthly life that they will experience many changes, but keep them walking on the path You have planned for them. May they recognize that Your path is unchanging. Amen.

**EXTRA STEPS** "He who is the Glory of Israel does not lie or change His mind; for He is not a human being, that should change His mind." 1 Samuel 15:29

**EXTRA STEPS** "Every good and perfect gift is from above, coming down from the Father of the heavenly lights, who does not change like shifting shadows." James 1:17

# 24

## Here Again

It's here. The cool, crisp air has finally arrived. I stepped out in a short-sleeved t-shirt and shorts, went across to the Crestwood track, walked one round and headed back. I wanted something a bit warmer on my arms and legs. Wonderful isn't it?

After the siege of hot weather through July and August, cool breezes and lower temperatures are a welcome break. I grabbed a light jacket and started again with a little quicker step than last week when even in the early morning the heat seemed to push me into the blacktop.

The weight of the hot summer has lifted. I can breathe deep again. Rejuvenated and refreshed, I anticipate walking even longer and farther in the next few mornings. I am still walking the same route, but the coolness of the morning, the rustling of the dry leaves and the geese honking across the lake encourage me that Fall is on its way.

I knew it would happen because God's world continues to work in the way He created it, but for a while, during those hot summer days, I had almost forgotten the caress of cool breeze, the whisper of dry leaves and the harsh honk of the geese that suggests a new season. I welcome the day with a prayer of thanksgiving for all the seasons and the joy each one brings, but today I thank God for my favorite season—Fall.

Life has its seasons, too. Seasons that weigh us down much like the physical heat of this past summer. Days of grief or physical pain or worry and concern for loved ones. Long periods of days when putting one foot in front of another seems difficult. Seasons when we are so burdened we forget the caress of children, the whisper of love and the sound of laughter.

If we trust Him, God takes us through that long hard season and brings us back to those times of joy. I am reminded this morning that He is still in control of His Creation, whether it is the seasons of the physical world or the seasons of our life and, I am thankful.

**My Prayer:** Lord, I thank You for each season, but this one is so welcome this year. I thank You for being with me during each season of the physical world, but I also want to thank You for the times You are with me in my seasons of hardship and grief. May I always remember that You are there in the good times and the bad. Amen.

**Extra Steps:** "Yet he has not left himself without testimony: He has shown kindness by giving you rain from heaven and crops in their seasons; he provides you with plenty of food and fills your hearts with joy." Acts 14:17

"We live in a fast-paced society. Walking slows us down."
—Robert Sweetgall

# 25

## Garbage

I hear the noise of the shifting truck gears and the grinding compactor as I step outside. It is Wednesday—garbage pickup day. All around my walking route I notice my neighbors have put out their trash. Some homes have two or three large cans overflowing with the refuse of their week. Others have only a little tied-up Walmart sack. The garbage men and I seem to be following the same route. I turn the corner; they turn the corner. I wave—they wave. This is not the first morning this has happened.

But this morning, it occurs to me how nice it is to have someone take away our refuse and rubbish each week. If only we could do the same thing with the garbage that shows up in our minds. I definitely would like to dispose of the trash that piles up in my thoughts each day.

My past week has been cluttered with vacation plans, family accidents and daily issues. Packed in around all this are the leftovers of the television shows, the books and the of proportion and each day's worries are enough for the day. (A brief Clella paraphrase of Luke 12:34). Our son-in-law is healing from his accident, and my worry will not speed his recovery. But so often, we carry this garbage from day to day until it piles up and interferes with our daily life.

I often forget that I do have a way to rid my mind of all these worldly troubles. Jesus told me "Come to me all you who are weary and burdened, and I will give you rest" (Mt. 11:28). So I walk into a new week with my burdens lifted.

**My Prayer:** Take away the clutter from my mind that I might see the plans You have for me. Help me each day to dump my cares on You and know that You will give me the clean thoughts I need for the day. Amen.

**Extra Steps:** "Carry each other's burdens" (Galatians 6:2)

**Extra Steps:** "Cast all your anxiety on him because he cares for you." (1Peter 5:7)

 **Extra Steps:**

# 26

## Weak Faith...Strong God

When I walk, I often reflect about how good God has been to our family. It is then I feel so weak in my faith, as I realize how many times I have failed to have faith in my God. For personal reasons, I am praying today for our grandson.

Our daughter's first child, this grandson, was the result of much faith and planning. Not my faith—I must confess. After filling out all the forms, answering all the questions, and passing all the tests and inspections, nothing was left for them but tears and frustration. Just wait and wait and continue to wait. Rather than just pass the time, they prayed and began to get ready for a child. Several years they waited, and they left the nursery door open. That open door was a symbol of hope to them, but to me as her mother it symbolized nothing but heartache and disappoint. My faith was not as strong as hers. But God works in His own time.

On a Friday morning, they were childless. On Monday they brought Eric home—a beautiful, baby boy. His nursery door was open and waiting for him. After long years, their prayers had been answered. God had provided.

Approximately ten years later, the door to the nursery

swung open again. Many foreign adoption stories filled my mind and none of them were good, but again the nursery door remained open as they anxiously waited for their Romanian daughter. While a representative of Save Eastern European Kids was visiting the Romanian nursery, the little girl who would become our granddaughter was brought from the streets of Bucharest to the door of the S.E.E.K. nursery. Timing of her arrival at the facility and the visit of the representative was no accident. God had provided our granddaughter.

Two children, both the obvious result of God's hand on our daughter and her husband as they came to the end of the painful road of infertility.

**My Prayer:** Thank You for continuing to provide for my family even when my faith is weak and I lose hope. Amen.

**Extra Steps:** "For I know the plans I have for you," declares the LORD, "plans to prosper you and not to harm you, plans to give you hope and a future." Jeremiah 29:11

"Good things are coming down the road, just don't stop walking."

— Robert Warren Painter Jr.

# 27

## Hearing

My devotion reading this morning was from Isaiah. He tells his reader, "Woe to the obstinate children," declares the Lord, "to those who carry out plans that are not mine" (Isaiah 30:1). I kept hearing that "Woe to the obstinate children" repeatedly while I walked. When I returned home, I went back to my Bible and finished the chapter. The part that really spoke to me was "your ears will hear a voice behind you, saying, 'This is the way, walk in it'" (Isaiah 30:21).

Isn't that an interesting thought! So many times we hear the voice behind us, but choose to walk *as an obstinate child.*" Time after time in my life God has quietly whispered, "this is the way", and I have turned left to walk another path. Or I have been at that crossroads and left the voice behind me as I walked the other way.

I think of times in my life when someone questioned my actions, and my quick response came. "I'll do it my way. This is what I want to do. This is where I want to go. No one can tell me what to do. I will make my own decisions."

It might not have been voiced aloud, but my inner voice was listening to "self" and not the voice saying, "this is the way; walk in it." So often we let the voice of "self" blare above that voice whispering in our inner ear.

Then I recall times when I listened to the loud voice of society and believed that "everyone else is doing it" so surely it is the way to walk. I turned and ignored the voice behind me although my heart recognized the voice.

Whether I have turned right or left, the times I have chosen to listen and obey that still, quiet voice in my ears have been those decisions I knew were right and pleasing to God.

Time after time God tells us in His Word, "Ask where the good way is and walk in it and you will find rest for your soul" (Jeremiah 6:16). I have found this to be true.

**My Prayer:** Help me, Lord, to listen more to Your voice and less to the voice of "self" and "society." Amen.

**Extra Steps:** " Whether you turn to the right or to the left, your ears will hear a voice behind you, saying, "This is the way; walk in it" Isaiah 30:21

"Thoughts come clearly while one walks." —Thomas Mann

# 28

## Do It Your Way

The little girl planted her feet. Her mother wanted her in the cart, but she wanted to walk. As I walked this morning, I thought of this scene I had witnessed yesterday. For a minute the mother insisted, and then shrugged as if to say, "Ok, have it your way." A few minutes later I noticed the child whining and wanting to ride. Mother smiled, reached down, hugged her and placed her in the cart—a typical parent/child scene that is re-enacted daily.

In his book *The Great Divorce*, C.S. Lewis writes, "There are two kinds of people: those who say to God, 'Thy will be done,' and those, to whom God says, 'All right, then, have it your way.'"[5]

How many times has God considered it necessary to say to us "All right, then, have it your way?" And we go our own way, doing our thing, only to come running back much like a crying child with a skinned knee or mashed finger. Like a sobbing child, we promise "I won't do it again." But like a child, we do.

His will is "not to gossip", but today I heard a story that I knew I needed to tell a friend, and I did. God said "all right, then, have it your way." As soon as the words exploded from my mouth, the damage was done. My argument with myself about "it was not really gossip" was so wasted. Now this evening I regret I repeated that story. I run to God with my cry of sorrow and repentance.

His will is "love your neighbor" but I don't feel like loving my neighbor. It's hot, I'm tired and there will surely be another day to visit. Besides, I'm just so busy…golf this morning, lunch at noon and then a trip to the grocery store and my time is gone. Even though my neighbor is shut in most of the time, surely she understands that I'm busy. God says, "All right, then, have it your way."

For some reason, I just don't feel too good about the day's activities even though I shot a good round of golf and lunch was extra-special. I rush to God with a promise to do better tomorrow.

His will is "build up and encourage one another." It is so easy to criticize those who are in charge of the organization, the town, the government, the church. Because it is easy, I often take that way and God says "All right, then, have it your way."

So I speak discouraging words to the women in the organization; I "bad mouth" our government leaders; I enlighten our church leaders with the age-old comment–"we don't do it the way we used to." I stop, hear my comments and then cry out to God for pardon. Yet again, I realize I have done it my way and my way just doesn't work.

As parents forgive their earthly children with hugs and assurances of love, so God reaches down and enfolds us in His loving arms. Because of His grace and mercy and the death of His Son on the cross, we can be forgiven for the many times we have done it our way first.

If only we as individuals, and our world as a whole, could realize that whether it is for the individual or for the marriage or for the government, God's way works. When we sincerely pray "Thy will be done", it is then God smiles down upon us as His children and surrounds us with His love.

**My Prayer:** Father in heaven, may I always pray "thy kingdom come, thy will be done." Forgive me for the many times I have tried my way first. Amen.

**Extra Steps:** "A perverse person stirs up conflict, and a gossip separates close friends." Proverbs 16:28

**Extra Steps:** "Without wood a fire goes out; without a gossip a quarrel dies down." Proverbs 26:20

It is no use walking anywhere to preach unless our walking is our preaching.
                                        —Francis of Assisi

# 29

## Another Season

The musty smell of harvest dust filters into the breeze. Farming families eat in fields; wives and children become errand boys and hired hands. The grain market and the weather report develop into the major news. The geese fly south again. Leaves fade into brilliant reds and golds and the harvest moon rises in the October sky. Fall festivals are rampant, school is in full swing and the high school football season dwindles to one game and the play-offs. Autumn has arrived in the Midwest.

Little chipmunks and bushy tailed squirrels invade my lawn. One little fellow struggles defiantly with the acorns falling among the leaves on our patio. As I step out quietly for my walk, I stop to watch his struggle. He finds them much more appealing than we do.

Across the way, the geese are strutting around the edge of Eads Lake, staking their claim to our neighbors' yards. Soon they will huddle, honk to one another and begin their journey across the sky. I pause to watch and listen as they rise into the blue October sky.

Farther around my circle, I notice that the neighbor on the corner has planted several mums. The full-blown bushes are swathed in blooms glowing in the light of the afternoon sun. I return to our house and note how all of my summer blossoms are beginning to fade to rusty brown. It is time to remove them from the pots and store them for next season.

Sitting with the sun soaking my shoulders, I reflect on the seasons of my life. I decide that each season has had its sunshine and its rain, its clouds and its storms. However, much like God's creation prepares this morning for the season ahead, I, too, continue to make preparation for winter. Of course, just as the seasons of nature come upon us rather quickly, so, too, do the seasons of life. It's almost Winter for me–in nature and in life. Am I prepared for the coming season?

Today's society seems so absorbed with today and the issues of the day that no preparation is made for the coming season. Planning and preparation are a part of God's plan. He has made plans for us in this life, "I know the plans I have for you…"(Jeremiah 29:11) and for eternity "I go to prepare a place for you" (John 14:3). Yet, we need to prepare for both. Perhaps I need to slow down, take a deep breath, and prepare for winter.

**My Prayer:** Lord, slow me down as I walk with You through this life. Help me to realize I need to take time to notice the small things You have prepared for me to do and not become so involved in "busyness" that I neglect the little things of life that are so important. Amen.

**Extra Steps:** "For everything there is a season, a time for every activity under heaven." Ecclesiastes 3:1

# 30

## Getting Ready

Angrily swishing his bushy tail, the little brown squirrel clings to the bottom branch and chatters nosily as I move the grill into the garage. The cardinal that I haven't seen for several days makes one last swoop at the fallen seed beneath the empty feeder. Acorns bounce across the patio as the wind whistles through the big oak tree in our back yard. Several little chipmunks peek out to see what is causing all the confusion. Everything seems to be getting ready for winter.

We, too, are preparing for our winter journey to Florida. Yesterday we stopped the mail and today will be the last day for the evening paper. We have made a list of our business information for our family and have told them where all the keys are located. As always before we leave, we will eat with our grandson and his wife, hug them one more time and shed that small tear I have each time I leave.

Even though I want to go and look forward to my Florida home, that final hug always brings a lump to my throat and a tear to my eye. These young people are so precious to us, but they have their lives and we have ours. Our preparation of the past few days is finished. We pull out the drive, turn the corner and start for our "other home."

It is much the same with our earthly life. As Christians, we have this earthly home. We enjoy it so much. Some of our family have already left, but many of them, especially the younger ones still surround us with their love. The church home we have been a part of for more than fifty years is familiar and we enjoy their love.

We are aware that we have another home, and as the winter of our life approaches, we begin to make specific preparations to go there. Anticipation fills our hearts, even though a small tear sometimes appears as we realize we will leave family behind. However, we have taught them what to do when we are not here for them. They have the direction of God's Word, and we have told them where the keys are.

We started preparing to leave the day we were baptized. Each time we read our Bible, attended a worship service, helped a friend, taught Scripture to our children, praised our God and loved our neighbor we were preparing for our heavenly home.

As we come closer to the time to go, we double check to make sure we have done all we should do. We don't want to leave anything undone that might cause a problem for those who are left to watch over earthly things, but neither do we want to miss the journey.

Getting ready to leave is the important part. Jesus said that he was going to prepare a place for us so we are assured that the home at the end of the journey is already waiting. We just need to make sure we have done everything we need to do before we leave.

**My Prayer:** God, please make us aware that each day we are preparing for the journey we will make at the end of this life. Give us the knowledge and the wisdom to make all the necessary preparations to live with You in eternity. Amen.

**Extra Steps:** "And if I go and prepare a place for you, I will come back and take you to be with me that you also may be where I am." John 14:3

### Prepare to Walk

- Ensure you are wearing appropriate footwear.

- Take your car to a park if it's too far away to walk;

- Some cities have bike boulevards or walking paths that are relatively flat and well-maintained.

- If you won't be tempted by the stores(shopping), shopping malls are also good locations for walking around.

- If you live near a large body of water, the shoreline can be a nice, relaxing place

- If indoor exercise is your thing, use a treadmill set to a slow speed for walking.

**Extra Steps:**

### 481   To the Work!

# 31

## A Child Again

Today I remembered that it was my turn to write the devotion for our on-line writers' group—The Kindred Hearts. Actually it was due on Monday morning, but I had forgotten it was my turn until I was reminded later in the week. Our verses for this group of devotional thoughts have been Revelation 21:4-7.

This has been one of those days when I can't seem to find enough hours for all I want to accomplish. So when I sat at my computer to write, I wrote these thoughts. Perhaps you too have felt this way at some time during your walk through life. May you turn the corner on these feelings as these words encourage and bless you in your walk with Him

### I WANT TO BE THE CHILD

To be someone's child again…
Some days I don't want to be the parent,
I want to be the child.
Some days I don't want to be the teacher,
I want to be the child.
Some days I don't want to be the nurse,
I want to be the child.

Some days I don't want to be the sitter,
I want to be the child.
Some days I don't want to be the coach,
I want to be the child.
Some days I don't want to be the adult,
I want to be the child.
Some days I don't want to be the narrator,
I want to be the child.
Some days I don't want to be me,
And on those days I remember,
I am God's child
And that is enough.

**My Prayer:** Lord, help me to remember I am Your child and I can always turn to You for help in any situation. Amen.

**Extra Steps:** "… and I will be their God and they will be my children." Revelation 21:7

### Ways to Be a Kid Again

1. Make a silly face at a stranger
2. Eat ice cream for dinner.
3. Go to bed early.
4. Hang out with your friends. Kids have play dates.
5. Color or draw something.
6. Try to say the alphabet backwards. Kids are great at crazy tasks.
7. Have a race.
8. Skip down the hallways at work.
9. Wear what you want.
10. Try a handstand.

*Paraphrased from Huffington Post/ Tara Phelps

# 32

## Home

We have made our annual move to Florida. It takes me a few weeks to make the transition. Not necessarily the weather, but also the home. What I think I have, I don't have and what I think I don't have, I have. Nothing seems to be in the right place, and I hunt for the sugar and find the salt.

I meet people I have known for several years and can't remember their name. Of course they call me by name and inquire about my health. I fake it until I can make an association with the face and the name.

Total confusion for a few days, but I adjust. It happens each year and will be the same when we return to Illinois. I am blessed to live in two places, but find myself being slower to adjust each year.

When I walk, people greet me with "Welcome Home, so good to see you. How have you been?"

I anticipate this each morning for the first few days. It is always a good feeling to know people are genuinely glad to see you.

As I walked this morning, I began thinking about heaven. As the birthdays go by, I find I think more about heaven and family and friends I plan to see there. Perhaps my thoughts of heaven occur because of the recent change in my environment, or maybe it is because when the holidays begin we go back to Edgar County, which is always home.

Whatever the reason, I have had heaven on my mind. Isn't that the name of a song? If it isn't, it should be. This morning I realize this is what will happen when I get inside heaven's gates.

I will walk in the light of the Son, and people I haven't seen for so many years will be glad to see me. They will call out as I enter "Glad to see you"! As I walk, I will see Jesus and He will smile and be glad to see me. I want to hear him say, "Well done good and faithful servant."

And the people there will call me by name, and I will know them. There will be no aching bodies, no dimming eyesight, no tears, no worries about the economy, no concerns about our children or our grandchildren, no heartache—just peace.

I finished my walk this morning and thanked God for His promise of a new life after this one. I love life here on earth, but I always know there is no comparison to what I will experience in heaven.

**My Prayer**: Lord, for all who read this today may they too have the assurance that someday we can greet each other in heaven. Amen.

**Extra Steps:** "He will wipe every tear from their eyes. There will be no more death or mourning or crying or pain, for the old order of things has passed away." Revelation 21:4

# 33

# Hitting the Wall

H itting the wall" is an expression often used by runners. Of course, a technical definition can be found in Wikipedia or any slang dictionary. For the common athlete "hitting the wall" refers to the moment when a person feels he/she cannot physically go any farther. Going on often takes them to a higher level, or at least, one is able to finish.

I have been quite lax about my walking schedule in the past few months. Many excuses and a few legitimate reasons, but my walking and thus my energy and stamina have deteriorated. I told myself that November I would be the date for me to begin again. By then we would be in our Florida home, and the weather would be better. By then, I would feel better. By then, I might have lost a few pounds.

Today it is November 1, and we are settled in our Florida residence, so I walked. Pulling on my old tennis shoes I started briskly on the route I have walked for several years. The first ten minutes went well, then my breathing became labored, my legs began to feel rubbery, and my heart was pounding. Fifteen minutes and I had hit the wall.

I told myself to keep moving even if I didn't cover

the entire route. Just one foot and then the other. I am proud to say I finished and plan to walk again tomorrow.

As I collapsed in my lawn chair to rest, I began to think about other times when I have "hit the wall," especially in my spiritual life. At different times in my sixty-five years of Christian walking, I have become so tired that I felt I couldn't go on and it wasn't really worth it. When I continued the walk, whether it was Bible Study, teaching a class, leading Vacation Bible School or writing a devotion, I have pushed on past the wall and found myself revived and rewarded.

**My Prayer:** Lord, help me when I feel as though I have done all I can do to realize that with Your help I can go on to the next level of service. Amen.

**Extra Steps:** "Therefore, since we are surrounded by such a great cloud of witnesses, let us throw off everything that hinders and the sin that so easily entangles, and let us run with perseverance the race marked out for us." Hebrews 12:1

**Extra Steps:** I encourage you to walk on past the wall.

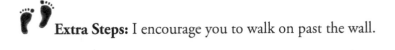

"Once you learn to quit, it becomes a habit…. KEEP GOING!!"
                    —Anonymous

# 34

## I Can Do It Myself

It began as such a simple thing—probably a pulled muscle. I didn't pay much attention at first – it was such a minor thing. A week or so later the pain became more concentrated. I continued to walk even though I limped by the end of my walk. I still ignored it.

Then it began to interfere with my daily plans. I began to wonder if perhaps I needed to check into it, but of course I didn't. When I started to limp and had to entirely quit walking, I decided maybe I should talk to someone about it. Not the doctor of course, only my friends.

I thought I could handle this with some time and a few pain pills. When I was no longer able to play golf, I decided to make a doctor's appointment. The doctor said tests and a specialist would be necessary.

If I had gone to the doctor earlier, the healing process could have begun much sooner. Now, six months later, the pain has become a part of each day. Epidural shots and exercise may finally conquer the problem.

Aren't we the same way about sin in our lives? It starts as such a small thing—a tiny streak of envy, a short minute of greed, one little lie, a moment of gossip. No need for us to give attention to such minor matters. Everyone has these moments, and our Christian walk is still strong and steady.

After awhile that first envious moment becomes full-blown coveting, the moment of greed takes precedence in our business practices, the little white lie blossoms into numerous cover-ups for the first lie, and the tidbit of harmless gossip is now interfering with someone's life. We start to limp in our Christian walk.

Our Bible study and prayer life are neglected, but we feel that whatever our problem we can take care of it. No need to bother the Lord about such a simple thing as a little lie. Besides, it didn't hurt anyone and made our friend feel better for a time. Of course, it became necessary to cover-up with another small falsehood, but it is all taken care of now. Nothing too drastic became of it.

Yes, the little moment of greed may have lost me a new friend, but some people get their feelings hurt so easily and the extra work seemed really needed. Anyone would have done the same thing. Why keep worrying about it?

Soon our friends are aware that something is wrong in our walk with the Lord. Someone mentions our absence from the worship service. Another Christian friend confronts us about the strain in an old relationship. Then a true friend exemplifies the love of Christ and confronts us with our "Christian limping".

As I finally went to the doctor for my physical pain, we realize we need to go to the Lord for help. We confess our sin. We make time for Him. We begin to study His Word. We pray. We are on the right path again. Healing begins and our "limp" is corrected for now.

We are again walking comfortably with our Lord and looking forward to what is around the corner in our service to Him.

**My Prayer:**  Lord, I want to remember that without You I am nothing. Forgive me for allowing Satan to convince me I can heal myself. Thank You for giving me friends to remind me of Your love and forgiveness. Amen.

**Extra Steps:** "I am the vine; you are the branches. If you remain in me and I in you, you will bear much fruit; apart from me you can do nothing." John 15:5

**Extra Steps:** "But he said to me, "My grace is sufficient for you, for my power is made perfect in weakness." Therefore, I will boast all the more gladly about my weaknesses, so that Christ's power may rest on me." 2 Corinthians 12:9

"It helps to have a friend like you to walk along the road with. Otherwise, who would point out to me when I'm going in the wrong direction? We may not be knowing where life is leading, but we have each other along the way. Who can ask for anything more?"
—Unknown

# 35

## Evening Walk

I watch the golden rays melt into yellow, fade blue, dissolve into pink and then bright orange as the sun slips into the blue of the horizon. It is gone—leaving only faded pink streaks dissolving into the silver gray of the Florida evening. As I walk slowly toward the fading glow, the warm breeze slacks off and stillness envelops the evening.

The time between sunset and dark called dusk surrounds my path, and I slow my pace to enjoy the calm at the end of the day. So often I am too busy, too tired, or too lazy to find that quiet time just before the dark of night.

When I do find time for an evening walk, many of my neighbors greet me, and we discuss the events of the day and our personal blessings and concerns. Just this evening, I chatted with a friend about granddaughters (hers and mine) and the heartaches and disappointments they must face as they begin jobs and marriages and families. It is good to share these mutual concerns.

Jesus told us to "share one another's burdens" and Paul told us "to encourage one another." My friend and I agreed that these issues are a part of maturing, and our granddaughters are both able to handle their situations.

Reassured, I turn the corner and head toward home. Darkness has fallen and the damp air of the evening feels refreshing after the heat of the day. Refreshed and ready for the night, I enter the kitchen, brew a cup of tea and relax for the evening. My life gets so bogged down with the day to day living that a slow walk at sunset, a visit with a friend and time of reflection is as uplifting to my spirit as it is to my body.

**My Prayer:** Thank You God for this time at the end of the day to reflect on the things you have done for me. Thank You for friends who share and for the freedom I have to walk in your wonderful creation and experience the refreshment it brings to my body and spirit. Amen.

**Extra Steps:** "Carry each other's burdens, and in this way you will fulfill the law of Christ." Romans 12:12

**Extra Steps:** "Come to me, all you who are weary and burdened, and I will give you rest. Matthew 11:28

# 36

## What's For Sale

As I finished my walk, I found myself thinking about the estate sale of two sisters we had attended recently. I knew nothing about their lives, but as the auctioneer's sales' patter rang through the loud speaker, a shudder of melancholy passed though me. Two lives displayed on long tables under striped tents, lining the perimeter of a half-acre field. All I knew about their lives is displayed here in this open field on a Saturday afternoon.

I stopped at a yard sale this morning and sifted through some items in a large box, slid the hangers back and forth on the metal clothes rack and flipped through several old books. Nothing there that really appealed to me, but I enjoyed digging though someone else's stuff.

Thinking about these different sales and the lives reflected, I considered how often we judge someone's life by the material possessions left behind. Frequently, we place such value on our earthly possessions-our home, our business, our diamond rings-that we lose sight of the truly valuable possessions of life.

Many work diligently to leave their children a profitable business, but leave no memories of spoken love and spiritual caring. Others scrimp for the education of their children and grandchildren, but neglect teaching them about God and his love for them.

Even if our material possessions are displayed for sale as a way to divide our estate this is not really significant. It is important that our heirs will have memories of our displays of love and a knowledge and desire for the word of God as a part of their inheritance.

**My Prayer:** I pray the inheritance I leave my children is a desire to study and live God's Word. May they cherish the memories of love in our family, and remember Christ and His love for them. Amen.

**Extra Steps:** "Do not store up for yourselves treasures on earth, where moths and vermin destroy, and where thieves break in and steal. But store up for yourselves treasures in heaven, where moths and vermin do not destroy, and where thieves do not break in and steal. For where your treasure is, there your heart will be also." Matthew 6:19-21

# 37

## Why Can't I Do Better

Why is it that we seem to fight the same battles? I can always relate to Paul who wrote to the Rome church, "I do not understand what I do, for what I want to do I do not do, but what I hate I do" (Romans 7:15). I am tired of walking each morning. Even though I know exercise is good for me, and I feel better both mentally and spiritually when I walk each day, I have missed several days, and I am not pleased with myself.

I am struggling with discipline—not of others, but of myself. I find that it is easier to rationalize or blame someone else when I fail to do that which I know may be difficult. I have written before about procrastination and lack of discipline, but still I find myself trapped with the same excuses and walking the same path time after time.

It is in these moments that God's Word comes back again. "For the Spirit God gave us does not make us timid, but gives us power, love and self-discipline" (2 Timothy 1:7). It is the self-discipline part I intend to memorize.

I must remind myself often that I have the power to discipline myself. Some translations read "sound mind"

95

rather than self-discipline. Some use self-control, and one reads "wise discretion" (which I rather like), but whatever the translation the meaning is clear. I have the power through the Holy Spirit to control myself.

With the help of the Spirit, I can discipline my mind and my body. I need not be timid for I have the power to overcome my desire to speak harshly or to judge quickly. I have the power to discipline my physical desires for food I don't need and exercise I do need. My power is in the strength of the gift of the spirit of love and self-discipline.

**My Prayer:** And so again this morning, Lord, I pray for the power to discipline myself to walk the road that has been set before me. Amen.

**Extra Steps:** "I do not understand what I do, for what I want to do I do not do, but what I hate I do." Romans 7:15

**Extra Steps:** "For the Spirit God gave us does not make us timid, but gives us power, love and self-discipline" 2 Timothy 1:7

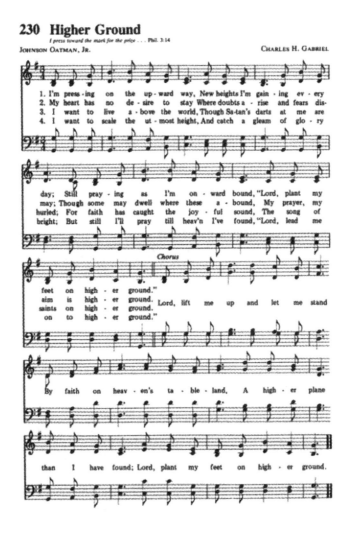

**Extra Steps:**

# 38

## Our Veteran Granddaughter

Written in 2013, but I wanted to include something for our Veterans and thought of this as I was compiling these devotions. Lauren returned home safely, and we now enjoy her Facebook posts as they are often pictures of her sweet children. I return to this post many times and am always blessed.

I walk this morning in the early Florida sunshine and pray for our granddaughter in Kuwait. I pray for her friends who serve with her and the family and friends who wait for their return.

At church yesterday a special service of beautiful music was presented for our veterans and the people who are serving now. Many around me wiped tears and some sat with bowed heads as we listened to "for spacious skies and amber waves of grain". And I asked "why?"Again this morning, I question.

I go to check my Facebook posts when I arrive home. There is my answer. She has given it to me on her post of the day. This is why she serves and why each of them serve and have served in the past. For us.

They sacrifice time and sometimes life for us, for this way of life. They serve so that we can speak freely about the government, about Obamacare, about Presidential elections, about anything we are not happy with at this time.

What a privilege it is to live in this country with all its blessings and yes, all its faults. So I say THANK YOU to all who have sacrificed and are sacrificing today.

To Lauren and Scott (her husband)..We love you and thank you for your service.

*Lauren's Facebook Post     11/11/13     Veterans' Day*

*"This is why I serve. For Pailynne and for her little sister Lola- whom I haven't met yet because I've been deployed. There are a thousand other reasons why but these are the two that are the first and last on my mind when I consider why I do this. Every Veteran has a story, has a reason for why they do what they do. There is an unthinkable sacrifice behind their story- consider that today. Consider their story...they are remarkable! To my brothers and sisters in arms- past and present- Thank You. It is an honor to serve alongside you."*

**My Prayer:** I pray I never forget how privileged I am to live in this country with my friends and family. May I always remember what sacrifice has been made by men and women before me that I can have this freedom. Amen.

**Extra Steps:** I urge, then, first of all, that petitions, prayers, intercession and thanksgiving be made for all people; for kings and all those in authority, that we may live peaceful and quiet lives in all godliness and holiness.
1 Timothy 2:1-2

# 39

## Try to Listen

It's a new year. I walk in Florida sunshine and praise God. At my age I should be thankful that I am busy and have the ability and health to go and do all the things I want. However, this year I want to be a bit more silent and listen to God in case He is whispering to me.

It is my plan to increase my walking time because it is then that I hear God. I find myself better prepared for my day if I have first exercised my body and at the same time exercised my mind. My Father knows what I need for the day. I need to talk, but even more He may be telling me to listen. Below are the "rules" I have written for myself as I turn this corner. Perhaps you, too, need to "hear".

**RULES FOR LISTENING**

1. **Choose a Scripture verse to think about while I walk.** This week I think I will finish up the week with "For I know the plans I have for you, they are plans for good and not for disaster, to give you a future and a hope" (Jeremiah 29:11).

2. Have **specific people in mind to pray for** as I walk. Make

a list if I can't remember.

3. Give a moment to offer **thanks and praise.** Make a list if necessary.

4. Attempt to **clear my mind** of all the details of the upcoming day. Sometimes I can use this time to prioritize my activities of the day. Getting my head straight at the beginning of the day is a good practice.

5. Accept what appears to be **God's will**. Test it against your own feelings and knowledge and the circumstances of the day.

**My Prayer:** I want to listen and then follow what You would have me do. Help me to clear my mind to hear Your message. Amen.

**Extra Steps:** "He says, "Be still, and know that I am God..." Psalm 46:10

 **Extra Steps:**

# 40

# The Second Mile

I began making excuses even before I reached the corner where I normally turn. My major excuse was the heat. My shirt was already damp and beads of perspiration glowed on my arms. I have been increasing my distance recently so I felt I could skip the second mile.

No one but me needs to know I didn't turn the corner. One day doesn't really matter. So, I didn't walk the second mile. I didn't even look that way when I arrived at the corner street sign. I went on my way toward home and really didn't think about it anymore.

Until this morning when I began to walk and realized how easy it was to walk by the corner where I turn for the second mile. It is still hot and all the excuses I gave myself the last time are still valid, so again I skipped the second mile.

It's much the same way in life isn't it? We go the first mile with our friend in need-give them an encouraging word, a pat on the back, a minute or two of our time. But if they need more, we can't seem to go around that corner. It's too hot to mow the elderly neighbor's yard; you don't have time to visit the shut-in down the street; you helped the young mother yesterday so surely she doesn't expect your help again this week.

Soon, all the reasons we give ourselves for not going that extra mile for those around us become a part of our daily thinking. What bothered us for a day or two is no longer a problem. I realized after a few days that my physical walking needed not only the extra mile but even more if I was going to sustain my physical stamina.

Help us to realize that the same is true in our relationships with the people around us. In Matthew 5, Jesus told his listeners "if someone asked us to go a mile, we are to go two." It is only when we go the extra mile that we become spiritually stronger and able to serve our family, our community and our Lord.

**My Prayer:** Lord, Let me remember to go that second mile. Give me wisdom to realize when a person or situation needs me to go on down the path with them. Amen.

**Extra Steps:** "If anyone forces you to go one mile, go with them two miles." Matthew 5:41

# Endnotes

1. Thomas, B.J. *Home Where I Belong*. Chris Christian. Myrrh Records, 1976.

2. *The Message*. Copyright © 1993, 1994, 1995, 1996, 2000, 2001, 2002. Used by permission of NavPress Publishing Group.

3. Warren, Rick (2002). *The Purpose Driven Life*. Michigan: Zondervan.

4. Longstaff, William, D. *Take Time to be Holy*. Public Domain, 1882.

5. Lewis, C.S. (1945) *The Great Divorce*. Geofrrey Bless. UK.

# About the Author

Clella Camp, a retired secondary English teacher, exhibits her ability as an instructor in these inspirational and impressive devotionals. Clella and her husband, Frank, are members of the Bell Ridge Christian Church in rural Paris, Illinois. During the winter, they reside in Florida and attend Liberty Baptist Church in St. Petersburg, Florida. Clella and Frank have been married sixty-one years and are parents of two children, four grandchildren and four great-grandchildren.